The **ESSENTIALS**® of

Management
Consulting

Sai Kolli, Ph.D.
Lecturer
School of Management
University of Texas at Dallas

Research & Education Association
61 Ethel Road West
Piscataway, New Jersey 08854

THE ESSENTIALS®
OF MANAGEMENT CONSULTING

Printed in the United States of America

Library of Congress Catalog Card Number 99-71130

International Standard Book Number 0-87891-260-6

ESSENTIALS is a registered trademark of
Research & Education Association, Piscataway, New Jersey 08854

WHAT "THE ESSENTIALS" WILL DO FOR YOU

This book is a comprehenensive and concise review of the findings in the field.

It is a handy reference source.

It condenses the vast amount of detail characteristic of the subject matter and summarizes the **essentials** of the field.

It will thus save hours of research and preparation time.

The book provides quick access to the important facts, principles, procedures, and techniques in the field.

Materials needed for this subject can be reviewed in summary form – eliminating the need to read and reread many pages of reference materials. The summaries will even tend to bring detail to mind that had been previously read or noted.

This "ESSENTIALS" book has been prepared by experts in the field, and has been carefully reviewed to assure accuracy and maximum usefulness.

Dr. Max Fogiel
Program Director

CONTENTS

Chapter 13
PROJECT MANAGEMENT—PLANNING AND CONTROL

Chapter 14
PROJECT MANAGEMENT—DOCUMENTATION AND PRESENTATIONS

Chapter 15
CONSULTING PROCESS—CONCLUSION

Chapter 16
CONSULTANT MANAGEMENT—CONSULTING COMPANY BUSINESS PLAN

Chapter 17
CONSULTANT MANAGEMENT—MARKETING CONSULTING SERVICES

Chapter 18
CONSULTANT MANAGEMENT—FINANCE

Chapter 19
CONSULTANT MANAGEMENT—ASSIGNMENT MANAGEMENT

Chapter 20
CONSULTANT MANAGEMENT—CONSULTANT DEVELOPMENT

Chapter 21
CONSULTANT MANAGEMENT—ETHICAL AND LEGAL ASPECTS

Chapter 22
COMPANIES AND CAREERS IN MANAGEMENT CONSULTING

CHAPTER 1

Introduction to Management Consulting

From a functional point of view, consulting refers to the provision of help with the content, process, or structure of a task or series of tasks, where the consultant does not perform the task on a regular basis but, instead, helps those who do perform it regularly. Management consulting is a way of assisting organizations and managers with management practices.

From a professional point of view, management consulting is an advisory service provided to client organizations by specially trained and qualified individuals who, in an objective and independent manner, assist with the identification and analysis of management problems, recommend solutions to these problems, and often participate in the implementation of those solutions.

1.1   Need for Management Consulting

The main objective of management consulting is to improve the performance of a client organization in areas such as profitability, quality, product, and service. Organizations use management consulting services for the following reasons:

1.   to rectify a situation where performance has deteriorated (*progressive problem*); and

1

2. to create a totally new situation (*creative problem*).

A *progressive problem* arises when an improvement in performance is required. Procedures that do not keep pace with changes in the organization hinder productivity. A consultant is expected to examine the current conditions, determine necessary adjustments to the procedures, and to train and sell the staff affected by an improved procedure. For example, the production of a manufacturing department may have deteriorated due to poor employee morale. These problems are not well structured and difficult to solve. A consultant suggests a set of actions to management that will correct the situation and help restore productivity.

A *creative problem* arises in a situation where there is no urgent problem or deteriorated situation, but where an opportunity for new actions or strategies is sought, such as finding new areas of business, developing products/services, or forming alliances with other organizations.

Organizations seek assistance from consultants rather than completely addressing the problems themselves, because consultants:

1. provide independent and unbiased recommendations;
2. provide new ideas and approaches;
3. possess skills and extensive experience with similar problems; and
4. supplement the skills of the client organization's employees.

1.2 Consulting Process

The consulting process involves the participation of the consultant and client in an activity aimed at identifying, defining, and solving problems, and then implementing the necessary procedures in the client organization. The process begins when the relationship is established and ends when the consultant completes the work and leaves the client organization. The consulting process is divided into five phases.

1. *Entry*—The first contacts between the consultant and client,

2

discussions and clarifications of their respective roles, preliminary analysis and preparation of a problem-solving plan, and negotiation of a consulting contract.

2. *Data collection and diagnosis*—This phase involves fact finding and analysis. Detailed data is collected on important aspects of the problem and examined. Insight gained in this phase helps in the generation of solutions.

3. *Solution development*—The generation of potential solutions, evaluation of alternative solutions, selection of the best solution, preparation of a plan for implementing the solutions, and presentation of a proposal to the client.

4. *Implementation*—Proposals made in the earlier phase start becoming a reality in this phase. Changes to the original design or plan may take place. If the client desires to handle the implementation completely without the help of a consultant, the consultant leaves at the end of the previous phase.

5. *Conclusion*—This stage involves the evaluation of the results after implementation. This may be followed by additional activities or future contracts. After these activities are completed, the consulting assignment is terminated by mutual agreement.

1.3 Project Management

The consultant and client interact with each other through a project, such as a billed telephone conversation on a large and complex project. Projects vary widely in scope and complexity and need to be managed effectively. Project management involves several steps.

1. *Proposal process*—This refers to the development of a proposal that offers consulting service to the client. There are different types of proposals, each requiring careful organization of the contents. This process ends with the presentation of the proposal to the client and follow-up.

2. *Planning and control*—This part of project management refers to the preparation of a plan that provides the client organization with the deliverables within cost, material, and time

constraints; execution of the plan; monitoring of project progress; and control of the project to ensure successful completion.

3. *Documentation and presentations*—This refers to all activities, progress reports, and project revisions. These form the basis for scheduling and controlling the project.

1.4 Consultant Management

Consultant management refers to the management of a consulting organization. Consulting organizations deal with assignment management (doing work for the client) and consultant management (managing its business). Management consulting is a business activity. Marketing its service and financing its operation is accomplished with earnings obtained from providing services to clients for a fee. The important aspects of consultant management include:

1. preparation of a business plan for the consulting organization;

2. marketing of consulting services to obtain new business opportunities by contacting current clients, generating referrals, gaining visibility in the professional community, and actively pursuing potential clients;

3. financial management of the consulting organization—handling costs, fees, budgeting, etc.;

4. managing the assignments of consultants at the client organization;

5. managing an effective consultant development program to maintain sufficient skills and knowledge at all levels of hierarchy in the consulting organization; and

6. maintaining high ethical standards to keep the profession reputable and in concurrence with legal guidelines.

CHAPTER 2

Types of Consulting Services

There is a wide range of management consulting services. These services may be classified based on criteria such as size and expertise.

2.1 Generalist vs. Specialist

Generalist consultants deal with several areas of management and the interaction, coordination, and integration of different areas of management. Specialist consultants have an in-depth and up-to-date knowledge of the subject and the required skills to solve a problem. Large consulting organizations have both types of consultant. Some assignments are primarily in the general management area (such as corporate policy and strategy) and some are primarily in the specialized management area (such as inventory management and staff scheduling). Most projects require the *involvement and cooperation of generalists and specialists.* For example, *generalists* may be involved in preliminary diagnosis, negotiation with the client, planning and coordination of the assignment, and supervision of the assignment.

Some accounting firms have departments that provide in-house management consulting services. These departments draw expertise and the opportunity to obtain assignments from the parent organization.

2.2 Size

Organizations with more than 100 consultants may be considered large; those with 50–100 are medium; and those with less than 50 are seen as small. Large consulting firms deal with a wide range of clients and handle complex assignments. They tend to have special capabilities and have various teams that focus on different sectors and types of problems. Some large firms, such as McKinsey and Anderson Consulting, operate worldwide with offices in many countries. Most small and medium-size consulting firms deal with a specialized area or serve a particular sector. These firms are easier to manage and have a small, close-knit group of consultants.

Senior and experienced consultants who operate individually are referred to as sole practitioners. The primary responsibility of a sole practitioner is consulting. They generally consult for small organizations. The services of a sole practitioner are less expensive than a large consulting firm, since overhead costs are minimal. Also, large organizations may seek assistance from a sole practitioner on small assignments. Some university professors and researchers whose primary job is not consulting may be involved in consulting on a part-time or regular basis. The combination of teaching, research, and consulting has a positive impact on the success of the assignment. By the same token, former executives with hands-on experience can be expert consultants.

2.3 Sectoral Focus

Some consulting firms have the majority of their business in one sector, such as transportation or health care. Some firms have separate departments that focus on a particular sector. This focus may be a result of a strong knowledge base and experience in management, economics, technical aspects of the sector, and part of the marketing strategy.

2.4 Custom vs. Packaged

Consultants who offer services that are tailored to solve a client's particular management problem are called "custom" consultants.

"Package" consultants are those who offer a standardized solution for generic types of problems at different client organizations.

2.5   Internal vs. External

Consultants who are not full-time employees of a client organization are referred to as external consultants. Employees of an organization whose primary responsibility is to provide consulting services to departments within the organization are called internal consultants. Organizations that are large and offer diverse products and services have internal consultants, since they tend to have more management problems than smaller organizations. The advantages of internal consultants are economy, knowledge of the company, and constant availability. The advantages of external consultants are independent and unbiased viewpoints, experience with related problems and solutions with other clients, and new ideas.

CHAPTER 3

Consulting and Change

Change is a common characteristic of all management consulting projects. Therefore, a consultant should be aware of the change process and help those involved in the project to cope with change. Changes may occur at an organizational or an individual level.

Organizational change may deal with issues such as image of the organization, financial performance, types of employees, employee morale and performance, technology, types of products and their mix, and the legal structure of the organization.

Individual change may occur as a result of a change in work methods, technology, personal factors, etc. To adapt to changes in an organization, individuals have to acquire new knowledge and skills, absorb new and additional information, change work habits, modify values and attitudes, and handle new assignments.

3.1 Resistance to Change

Resistance to change may occur for a variety of reasons. Individuals who have experienced negative consequences from change or a great deal of unnecessary change tend to be suspicious of change. Some reasons for resistance to change include:

1. *Fear of the unknown*—Those who do not like uncertainty prefer an imperfect present to an unknown and uncertain future.

8

2. *Dislike of surprises*—Management decisions that bring about change tend to be resented if they come as a surprise to the employees.

3. *Opposition to imposed change*—Employees resent change that is imposed on them by management and about which they cannot express any views.

4. *Lack of conviction*—If employees are not informed about change and its purpose, they are likely to feel that the change is not needed.

5. *Fear of insecurity*—Employees may feel insecure about their ability to cope with change, to learn special skills, and improve their performance.

After the organizational change, employees who are established in the current workplace, methods, and relationships may be required to operate in a totally new environment. This can lead to considerable frustration and unhappiness and may result in poor employee morale and productivity.

3.2 Approaches to Change

There are four basic approaches for generating and implementing change in an organization.

1. *Planned change*—Involves proactive change, where organizations prepare themselves for changes that can be anticipated and minimize hasty changes made in an atmosphere of panic. There is a limit to the amount of change that can be absorbed by individuals and organizations. Therefore, the process of change should be planned and managed carefully.

2. *Imposed change*—Involves change in situations where the individuals affected by the change are not consulted or informed about the change. The change may be imposed from a position of power and may cause unhappiness and resentment among individuals affected by it. Management would impose a change in situations where lengthy discussions with individuals and affected groups are not possible (emergency

situations) or when discussions are not considered to be of major importance (change dictated by government/regulatory agencies).

3. *Participative change*—This approach to change is adopted when individuals want to know about changes that are being made and to influence these changes. While the participative approach to change is more time consuming than the imposed change, its effects are long-lasting and result in better employee morale.

4, *Negotiated change*—This is used as an approach when there are two or more individuals or groups involved in the discussion about change and related costs and benefits. This type of approach is necessary where the law stipulates that changes require the negotiation between management and employee unions.

3.3 Managing Change

Managing change refers to planning, implementing, and facilitating change in individuals, groups, and organizations. Change can be effectively managed if the organizational culture is supportive of it. Organizations that stimulate and reward innovation and creativity tend to have a positive attitude toward change and realize that change results in benefits to the organization. Also, organizations that have established programs of collecting ideas and suggestions from employees are receptive to change and understand that it is necessary to meet the organizational goals. Organizations should balance change and stability, define an optimal pace of change, and ensure that all employees understand that a certain amount of change is necessary to meet the goals of the organization.

CHAPTER 4

Types of Clients

Clients may be classified into various types; an understanding of the variety is useful in providing effective consulting service. Major corporations differ from small family businesses in management styles and problems; service companies differ from manufacturing companies in the extent of customer involvement in the operation.

4.1   Industry Differences

Manufacturing companies produce tangible products, require large investments in equipment, and carry inventory. Service companies deliver services that are intangible, require less capital for equipment, involve more labor, and have little or no inventory. The type of employees required in these two types of companies is different due to the different kinds of customers and variability in the expectation of each customer. Service organizations require employees with diagnostic and interpersonal skills, while manufacturing typically requires employees with special technical skills. For example, the issues faced by an auto manufacturer are often not similar to those faced by a hospital.

Certain industries operate in the presence of government regulations. For example, regulations can limit flexibility in changing pricing policies in an electric utility firm, or introducing new products in the case of a food and drug manufacturer.

Growth rate is another important classification criteria. Rapidly growing industries, such as electronic manufacturing, deal with major investments in research and development while other industries, such as steel producers tend to be more involved in cost cutting and performance improvement.

To provide the best possible service, an effective consultant makes an effort to identify, understand, and appreciate the uniqueness of each client.

4.2 Public Agencies

Local, state, and federal government organizations are subject to a set of laws, resource constraints, customer demands, and a decision-making process that is different from private organizations. A major difference is that public agencies have little or no competition and, therefore, there is little natural incentive to become more efficient. Unlike private agencies, they do not rise and fall with customer reaction. Also, customer reaction has little direct impact on the budget for these agencies. These agencies have a formal procedure for submitting proposals and preparing the contract. The process of payment for the consulting services is formal and rigid compared to private agencies.

CHAPTER 5

Roles of Consultants

Consultants interact with clients in a number of ways and their roles in the relationship depend on the situation, the consultant's style, and the expectations of the client. There are two basic types of roles for a consultant: a resource role and a process role.

5.1   Basic Roles

The *resource role*, also called the expert role and the content role, pertains to the role in which the consultant suggests to the client *what to change*. The consultant provides technical expertise, but does not get actively involved in the change process in the client organization. The resource consultant supplies information, conducts diagnosis, solves the problem, recommends changes or solutions, and advises in implementation.

The *process role* refers to the role in which the consultant suggests *how to change*, assists the client in the change process, and handles any related issues. A process consultant does not provide technical advice or solve problems but helps the client to diagnose and solve its problems.

These two roles are complimentary and mutually supportive. Some consultants are comfortable in both roles. A consultant may work with a client as a resource consultant on an assignment and demonstrate his/her technical expertise, and later work as a process consultant and help the client solve its problems.

13

5.2 Other Roles

A consultant may assume more roles than these two basic ones. Different situations may require the consultant to take one or more of the following roles.

1. *Advocate*—A consultant influences the client to choose a particular product or methodology for solving the problem.

2. *Technical expert*—A consultant uses technical skills and experience to define the problem and objectives, conduct diagnosis, solve the problem, and make recommendations. This is similar to a resource role.

3. *Trainer and educator*—A consultant designs the learning program, trains, and teaches the client. This type of consultant has the skills to develop training programs and help the clients learn.

4. *Collaborator in problem solving*—The consultant uses a co-operative approach in identifying, diagnosing, and solving the problem. The consultant's contribution is in maintaining objectivity and stimulating the process with his/her rich experience and skills.

5. *Fact finder*—The consultant is confined to collecting data and developing a database of facts.

CHAPTER 6

Skills for Effective Consulting

Skills that are important for effective consulting may be classified into three types:

1. *Consulting process skills*—Ability to understand the consulting process in solving business problems;

2. *Interpersonal and communication skills*—Personal attributes that make a consultant amiable with people and effective in accomplishing the goals of the project; and

3. *Technical skills*—Knowledge and experience in a technical subject.

6.1 Consulting Process Skills

Consulting requires certain skills that are unique to the industry--problem solving and an understanding of the consulting process.

It requires skills to:

1. examine the organization, understand the individuals and departments, assess the nature of power and politics, sift through the maze of detailed information, separate the causes from symptoms, isolate the important factors; and

2. use related business practices and creativity to suggest innovative solutions.

15

A consultant needs the ability to recognize and understand the dynamics of internal power and political relationships, and to use them to recommend change that meets the objectives of the assignment. A knowledge of the consulting process (entry, data collection, diagnosis, solution development, and implementation), types of clients, types of change and methods to influence and manage change, professional ethics, and an understanding of the consulting philosophy are necessary for effective consulting.

6.2   Interpersonal and Communication Skills

Since consulting involves dealing with people rather than machines, a consultant must have good communication and interpersonal skills. Personal attributes are as important as technical skills. A consultant with excellent technical skills but poor communication and interpersonal skills, and poor behavior and attitude, cannot be effective in an assignment. The consultant should be professional in attitude and behavior and should be sincerely interested in helping the client organization. Some important personal attributes are:

1. *Drive*—Self-confidence, courage, initiative, and perseverance;

2. *Communication*—Ability to listen, ability in both oral and written communication; ability to teach and train people; and the ability to motivate and persuade;

3. *Emotional maturity*—Ability to withstand frustrations, uncertainties, and work pressures, stable behavior, self-control at all times, ability to draw unbiased conclusions, flexibility and adaptability to changed conditions; and

4. *Behavioral*—Ability to anticipate and evaluate human reactions, ability to gain trust and respect, courtesy and good manners, tolerance and respect for others.

Messages that are communicated poorly lead to misinterpretation and misunderstanding, which may frustrate the client. An understanding of common barriers to effective communication in the consulting environment helps a consultant to deal with them or eliminate them. Some of the important barriers are:

1. *Inability to understand technical language*—The client may not understand a message if the consultant uses technical terms that are not familiar to the client.

2. *Poor organization of the material*—A message that lacks coherence and logical reasoning reflects the inability to structure and develop an idea. The client may lose interest in the material and question the credibility of the consultant. Adequate planning and preparation help in better organization and presentation of ideas.

3. *Information overload*—Presentation of more information than necessary to explain a topic may hamper effective communication.

6.3 Technical Skills

Consultants should have a thorough knowledge of their field of expertise (general management, marketing, or manufacturing). In addition, all areas of management consulting require skills such as design of questionnaires, basic statistics, and mathematics. Statistics should include sampling and probability concepts. The specialized areas should include financial analysis, product research concepts, and some knowledge in personnel recruiting.

CHAPTER 7

Client-Consultant Relationship

The client-consultant relationship refers to the collaboration between the client and the consultant. To avoid mistrust and misunderstanding in this relationship, expectations and roles of the client and consultant must be clearly defined and understood. The client's definition of the problem may be different from that of the consultant. Both should discuss and correct the initial definition of the problem and agree on a definition that is acceptable to both. Also needed is a clarification of the results expected from the assignment and how the results will be measured.

The consulting assignment involves a direct contact between individuals acting on behalf of their organizations. Therefore, the client-consultant relationship is personalized and the success of the assignment depends largely on the compatibility of the parties.

7.1 Collaboration

The extent of collaboration between the client and consultant may vary from assignment to assignment. However, there should be a spirit of cooperation and a shared desire to make the assignment a success. Collaboration is needed for the following reasons.

1. The client's staff cannot learn about the problem, its solution, and recommendations if they do not collaborate with the consultant. Learning through joint work is necessary to obtain benefits from the assignment.

2. Senior management in the client's organization may not be aware of the competence within the organization. Joint work with the consultant helps the client to uncover and mobilize their strengths and resources.

3. A consultant cannot perform certain tasks if there is no collaboration with the client. The client may refuse to provide critical information needed by the consultant to complete some tasks in the assignment.

4. Collaboration makes the client more committed to the project and more likely to accept the consultant's recommendations.

7.2 Influencing the Client

Individuals who participate in the client-consultant relationship are those who initiate the idea of bringing in a consultant, discuss the problem with the consultant, collaborate during the assignment, receive and review reports, and provide comments and recommendations to senior management.

Managers, supervisors, analysts, and liaison officers in the client organization may be involved in the assignment at various stages. Since the consultant comes in contact with a number of individuals from the client organization, s/he must try to understand the client organization and relationships between individuals and departments, identify and understand the person or department who "owns" the problem—who has the main interest in the success or failure of the assignment, the person who has the real power to make decisions related to the assignment, and whose direct collaboration is essential. The consultant explores the client system on a continual basis because there may be a change of individuals in the department during the process.

The consultant needs to influence individuals in the client organization to obtain information, gain confidence and respect, get cooperation, overcome any resistance, and to get proposals accepted and implemented. The following is a list of methods that can be used to influence the client to activate a productive relationship:

1. *Developing a joint vision*—A demonstration of enthusiasm and future scenarios of the organization if a certain course of action is taken. This method is effective in influencing a large group of people.

2. *Assertive persuasion*—The presentation of ideas and suggestions along with arguments and data in an effort to convince the client that the suggestions are appropriate and valuable to the client. This method is effective if the consultant is perceived as knowledgeable and capable of solving the client's problem.

3. *Demonstrating expertise and integrity*—A demonstration of technical expertise and practical experience to the client. During discussions with the client, the consultant can provide information on the latest developments in theory, techniques, equipment, and successful assignments related to the topic. Proposals and other reports submitted by the consultant that are superior in terms of techniques used and effectiveness of solutions will enhance the image of the consultant. Also, the consultant's behavior at work while collecting information, perseverance in finding a good method to solve the problem, making proper use of time, using tact in handling delicate matters, and commitment and integrity are all observed by the client. A productive relationship is possible if the client believes that the consultant has the necessary expertise, integrity, and commitment.

4. *Participation and mutual trust*—Creating an atmosphere of cooperation and shared responsibility for achieving a common goal. Methods include involving and recognizing the individuals in the client's organization by requesting their contributions and ideas, giving them credit for their ideas, and building on the ideas provided by them.

5. *Incentives*—Influencing the client by providing things that are desirable to him/her, such as recognition. A consultant can reward an individual from the client's organization through a public acknowledgment of competence, achievement, and contribution to the assignment.

CHAPTER 8

Consulting Process—Entry

Entry is the first phase of the consulting process. It starts with the initial contacts between the client and the consultant, and ends with the agreement and signing of a consulting contract. During the initial contacts, the client and consultant learn about each other; the client tries to be sure that the consultant is suitable for the assignment, while the consultant tries to learn about the assignment and the client to be sure that the consulting assignment is worthwhile.

The consulting process may involve a new assignment with a new client or a new assignment with a previous client. In the case of repeat business, the entry may be simpler than for a new business. However, individuals in the client organization may be different from those that the consultant dealt with in an earlier assignment. In general, the consultant is a stranger to the client organization. There may be anxiety, uncertainty, and mistrust in the initial relationship. Therefore, the contacts in the initial phase are more important than the later phases. Assignments are likely to be successful in the presence of mutual trust and empathy, a full agreement about the "rules of the game," and shared optimism.

8.1 Preliminary Contacts

The initial contacts may be initiated by either the consultant or the client. The client may initiate the contact by seeking consulting assistance from a particular consultant or may invite several consultants to

21

submit proposals. Typically, a client organization may need consulting assistance when it has performance problems or a special need. The client may seek a particular consultant because of services provided by that consultant in the past, the consultant's reputation, referrals, the consultant's publications, or participation in professional meetings. On the other hand, a consultant may make the initial contact through marketing efforts. This initiative may lead to an assignment if the consultant has adequate knowledge of the client, demonstrates that the client can improve performance, and provides information on services that can help the client.

The first meeting between client and consultant does not necessarily end in a contract. The consultant is still in the process of marketing the services and gaining the confidence of the client. Typically, the first meeting is between senior staff from the client organization and a team of members from the consulting firm whose primary responsibility is negotiating the scope of the assignment, resources needed, and other related aspects. However, some clients may not prefer this approach because they meet the best people (senior consultants) in the initial meeting, sign a contract, and then receive service from inexperienced consultants.

In the initial meetings, the client does not expect a solution to the problem, but familiarity with problems in the organization and the industry. Before attempting preliminary diagnosis of the client's problems, the consultant should become familiar with basic facts of the organization and industry: basic terminology, types of products and services, sources of raw materials, processes and equipment, competitors, business methods and practices unique to the industry, economic aspects, main problems of the industry, background of the senior executives of the client organization, etc. During these meetings, the consultant should encourage the client to do most of the talking and have them explain the problems, hopes, and expectations. The consultant should assess the client's needs and readiness to work with him/her.

After the initial meeting, if the consultant and client are interested in working together, other activities, such as preliminary problem diagnosis, follow. During a formal consultant selection process, the proposals are expected to be received in a standard format within a specified time period. The client then evaluates proposals submitted by various consultants and makes a selection. If there is no formal selection procedure, the client should inform the consultant about the selection procedure and the nature and type of proposal to be submitted. The client and consultant should also discuss and agree about charges for the preliminary diagnosis. In general, if the preliminary diagnosis requires a short period of time, the client is not charged for the service. However, preliminary diagnosis for a large and complex assignment requires considerable time and effort and, the client may be expected to pay for the service.

8.2 Preliminary Diagnosis

After the preliminary meetings, the client provides information about the problems and expectations to the consultant. The consultant then conducts a preliminary diagnosis of the problem to formulate an approach for handling the assignment.

The preliminary diagnosis is limited to quick data gathering and analysis to understand the problem, discussions with the client personnel, and a review of the problem from different perspectives (functional perspective and overall organization perspective).

8.3 Assignment Plan

Assignment planning includes the following steps:

1. *Problem identification*—The results from the preliminary problem diagnosis are used to prepare a description of the problem.

2. *Objectives and activities*—A list of objectives related to the problem and associated performance measures (economic, social, and nonquantitative) should be identified and presented. The nature and type of activities needed to complete the assignment also should be presented.

3. *Schedule of the assignment*—A list of all activities and phases of the assignment and their sequence should be provided. Also, the types of reports to be submitted at major milestones during the assignment should be mentioned. To moni-

tor the progress, various reports are prepared at the end of major phases of the assignment. These reports keep the client informed about the payment schedule and in the preparation of budgets.

4. *Roles*—The consultant recommends a style of consulting appropriate for the assignment and a description of the roles of the client. A carefully defined role document reduces or eliminates misunderstandings. The definition should clarify issues such as: What activities will be carried out by the consultant and the client? What data and documents will be prepared and by whom?

5. *Resource planning*—A list of activities and the roles of the client and consultant for various phases of the assignment help determine the resources required. Consultant resources include time, research material, administrative support, legal advice, and computing facilities. Client resources include data, computing facilities, business expertise, office facilities, and administrative support. A clear definition of resources and associated costs are required to avoid misunderstandings and wrong expectations.

8.4 Proposal

The assignment plan (discussed in the previous section) is described in a document called the proposal. It may also be referred to as a project proposal, project document, project plan, technical proposal, survey report, etc. A proposal is an important selling document and, therefore, it should be clear to the individuals from the client organization who were involved in the meeting with the consultant and to other individuals in the client organization. While some proposals are expected in a special format, most proposals contain the following basic sections.

1. *Technical*—Describes the consultant's assessment of the problem, any preliminary findings, and the assignment plan.

2. *Staffing and consultant background*—Provides names and profiles of the consultants who will be involved in the

assignment. Also includes description of similar work conducted by the consultant for other organizations.

3. *Financial*—Provides information on the fee for consulting services, provision for contingencies, and a schedule for fee payment.

The proposal document may be presented to the client along with an audiovisual presentation. Often, the client will be interested in reading the proposal before inviting the consultant for a presentation. Proposals are evaluated by the client based on criteria that are made clear in the preliminary meeting. The criteria generally include the consultant's experience, the assignment plan, and competence of the consulting staff proposed for executing the assignment. The client may like to receive the initial service from the consultant but may not be comfortable with some aspects of the proposal such as time, cost, and the tasks involved. The client may propose reducing or changing the tasks listed in the assignment plan or may undertake some tasks so as to reduce the time or costs. A consulting contract is prepared and signed after the negotiation of the proposal is completed.

8.5 Contract

The entry phase of the consulting process ends with the consulting contract. The purpose of this contract is to protect the interests of both parties, client and consultant, and to provide a clear orientation for the joint work. The consulting contract may be in one of three forms.

1. *Verbal agreement*—After reviewing the consultant's proposal, the client and consultant may reach a verbal agreement. This is not a common form of contract. It is used if the client and consultant trust each other, they are familiar with each other's terms of reference, the assignment is short, or the client and consultant have a prior working relationship.

2. *Written contract*—Some clients use a standard contract form and expect the consultant to prepare the necessary information for completing the form. Often, the consultant may use his/her format if the client does not have one. Due to legal

reasons or the policy of the client or consulting organization, a written contract is usually prepared and signed.

3. *Letter of agreement*—After reviewing the proposals and selecting a consultant, the client may send a letter of intent or agreement to the consultant indicating that he/she accepts the proposal and the accompanying terms of reference. Modifications to the proposal may be listed in the letter of agreement; the consultant sends a letter back to the client indicating whether or not the new conditions are acceptable.

The contract should also include a statement describing the normal conditions for executing the assignment and how to handle special unforeseen conditions. Since the nature and magnitude of the assignment may change, the contract should describe how such conditions will be treated. It may be better to prepare a contract for each major stage of the assignment, for example, a contract for the data collection and diagnosis part of the assignment and another contract for the implementation part of the assignment.

CHAPTER 9

Consulting Process— Process Development

A proposal is a plan and offer of consulting assistance that may be accepted or rejected by the client. It is a vital part of the consultant's sales effort. The likelihood of acceptance of a proposal depends on the content, format, presentation, and interaction between the client and consultant. A proposal may be considered effective if:

1. the focus is on the problems and needs of the client; it should indicate that the consultant has the competence to solve the client's problems and make effective recommendations;

2. the material is clear and precise;

3. the style is consistent throughout the proposal; and

4. the written material is enhanced with graphics such as diagrams, graphs, pictures, and flowcharts that make the proposal easily understandable and readable.

9.1 Proposal Cycle

The proposal includes the following steps.

1. *Initial opportunity*—This is the result of marketing and sales efforts of the consultant or the client's invitation to submit a proposal.

2. *Background research*—This is essential for preparing a good proposal. The consultant should study the problem, the personalities of people from the client organization who would be involved in the project, the client's management style, etc.

3. *On-site fact finding*—This is conducted after the background research to obtain additional information through on-site interviews. Employees in the client organization have a good knowledge of the working of the organization and problems, and often have good solutions for the problems. This exercise helps the consultant to learn more about the client and the problem and leads to a responsive proposal.

4. *Proposal presentation*—This involves preparation of a formal document that is submitted to the client.

5. *Submission and evaluation*—This is the final part of the proposal cycle and consists of submitting the proposal document and, in some cases, is supplemented by an audiovisual presentation. Depending on the client's personality and style, the proposal may be submitted at the client's location or the consultant's office. An appropriate time and location should be set up so that the client can give full attention to the proposal and understand that the consulting firm is interested in working on the project. This step is followed by evaluation of the proposal (and a selection if there are proposals from multiple consultants).

9.2 Proposal Content

A proposal document contains a title for the project and description of the problem; scope and nature of services to be provided; benefits from proposed services; amount of time required; fees and billing arrangements; staffing, client personnel, physical facilities, supplies, etc.; and references and profiles of the consulting staff assigned to the project.

The proposal should demonstrate the consultant's understanding of the problem. This is important since the client would not give the project to a consultant who does not have an understanding of the

28

problem. The proposal should include only those areas that are relevant to solving the problem. It should be based on the study of the problem and discussions with the client and include information on the number of people on the client's staff, volume of work produced, layout of facilities, equipment used, and the client's management style. It should explain how the consulting assignment will be conducted at the client's site and the consultant's office.

The proposal should list the consultants who will be working on the assignment and describe briefly their experience and how it relates to the project. The list should also include those who represent the firm on important issues. Based on this list, the potential client should be able to assess if appropriate resources have been assigned to the project. In addition to the information on the consulting staff, the consultant should provide information on the estimated time for completing the project, fees, and phases of the project and schedule.

One of the most important parts of the proposal is the description of the benefits that will be obtained from the consulting services. The consultant should avoid overestimating the benefits to the client and also should avoid providing an impression that the consultant benefits more than the client in the project.

The material in the proposal should address the following issues:

1. Consultant's understanding of the problem;

2. Work that the consultant proposes to do;

3. Method by which the consultant proposes to do the work;

4. Amount of time required for the proposed work;

5. Start and finish time for the project;

6. Fees to be paid by the client;

7. Consultant's qualifications for the project;

8. Consultant's reasons for offering assistance;

9. Resources that the consultant will use and the resources that are needed from the client;

10. Benefits that the client can expect; and

11. References that the client may contact for information on the consultant's competence.

9.3 Proposal Presentation

Proposal presentation is the final step in the proposal process, which may be considered a sales effort. For this sales effort to be successful, the proposal should address all the client's expectations. The presentation may be made by a single consultant or a team of consultants. The presentation team includes those who dealt with the client throughout the proposal process. Before presenting the proposal to the client, the presentation team should rehearse, with someone playing the role of the client, and emulate every circumstance that is likely to arise in the real presentation. This rehearsal is necessary since the proposal involves considerable time and cost to prepare; a poor presentation may result in a rejection and render all the effort worthless. A follow-up after the presentation is necessary to ensure that there is a clear understanding between the client and consultant. Follow-up meetings help to resolve any questions.

9.4 Types of Proposals

The proposals may be presented in various formats. Some of the common types of proposals are:

1. *Formal proposal*—Used for lengthy and complex projects that require several pages to describe the problem and the proposed work.

2. *Letter of understanding*—Used for short projects when both the client and consultant have a clear and complete understanding of the project. This letter provides a summary of the problem and the proposed work, and also states the time, fees, and level of cooperation needed for the project.

3. *Unsolicited proposal*—Prepared as a part of the marketing and promotion effort. If a study of the client organization indicates a performance problem or opportunity for new ventures, the consultant may submit a proposal suggesting consulting services to the client.

CHAPTER 10

Consulting Process— Data Collection and Diagnosis

This stage of the consulting process involves a thorough study of the problem faced by the client to identify the factors causing the problem. Another important task in this stage is to collect information to understand the relationship between various factors influencing performance problems. Observations and results of the diagnosis are used to develop solutions in the next stage of the consulting process (see Chapter 11). In certain cases where diagnostic work already identifies and explores possible solutions, it may be difficult to make a distinction between the diagnostic and solution development stages.

10.1 Plan for Data Collection

At the beginning of the data collection and diagnosis phase, a certain amount of data is available which was collected during the preliminary problem diagnosis in the entry stage. In the diagnosis stage, more detailed information is needed. The nature of data needed depends on the problem and objectives of the assignment.

An excessive amount of information is difficult to manage and may not be fully utilized in the assignment, and limited information may exclude information that would have helped in the diagnosis. The consultant and client should collectively define the:

1. *Scope*—This deals with the determination of whether to collect complete or limited information. In general, data that is relevant to the problem is collected.

2. *Amount of detail*—More detailed information requires more time and cost for data collection. At the beginning of the assignment, it may be difficult to determine the amount of detail required. Data could be collected in many stages. In its initial stage, data is collected in broad categories. Examination of this data indicates the need for detail in certain categories. Further examination of these categories helps identify areas that need further details.

3. *Time period*—The plan for collecting data also specifies the time period for which data will be collected. For example, to understand the performance of the sales department, data on sales figures may be required for three years to understand any patterns in performance. Time periods when there are exception events (such as labor strikes) should be excluded or the data for those periods should be adjusted appropriately. Also, time periods with major changes in operations, such as replacement of old equipment, should be examined separately from time periods with normal operations.

4. *Organization of data*—The data should be arranged in a format that is easy to tabulate. It should also be easily transferable into a computer file.

10.2 Sources of Data

Data is available internally (within the client organization or the consulting firm) and externally (such as industry and government reports). There are three basic types of sources:

1. *Records*—Data stored in a form that is readable, including reports, computer files, microfilms, pictures, etc.;

2. *Conditions*—Circumstances in the organization that can be observed and the results of the observation recorded; and

3. *People*—Information from the people working in the organi-

zation from their experiences, opinions, beliefs, impressions, and insights. This can be obtained by means of interviews and questionnaires.

10.3 Data Collection Methods

Following are some of the important techniques used for data collection:

1. *Document gathering*—This method involves collection of records that are available within the client organization. These records should be verified to make sure they provide accurate information. Records may exist in different departments that show different information about the same activity or measure. This data collection method requires less time and cost.

2. *Questionnaires/Interviews*—If the information is not readily available in reports, questionnaires or interviews are used to obtain the information. The consultant should determine the information needed, how it will be used, and how the answers will be summarized before designing the questionnaire. The questionnaire is useful in collecting information on a limited number of simple questions from a large number of people. If detailed information is needed and only a few people have the information, interviewing is a more appropriate technique. In addition to the direct replies to the questions, the consultant also receives comments, opinions, anecdotes, inferences, information on related topics, relationships, influences, etc.

3. *Observation*—This method involves the collection of information related to a process by observing it. This helps the consultant determine what is done, how it is done, who is doing it, when it is done, how long it is done, where it is done, and why it is done. Observations may be conducted while moving (walking in the department that is studied) or from a fixed location (interacting with people or using a camera). The interaction may involve asking questions about

33

a task or asking for detailed explanations of a certain task. Since people tend to feel uncomfortable under scrutiny, the consultant should explain the purpose of the observation and ensure that the tasks are performed at a normal pace and under good conditions.

10.4 Diagnosis

A clear understanding of the problem requires diagnosis, involving a great deal of probing, testing and evaluating, assessing the client's readiness for change, and the elimination of any human bias. Analysis begins with an attempt to correctly describe the reality, i.e., conditions and events and their causes, and evolves into a synthesis that involves drawing conclusions from the analysis and developing solutions.

Before the data is used for analysis, it is edited and organized. Editing involves checking the completeness of the data, verifying the clarity of recording and presentation, eliminating and correcting errors, and ensuring that uniform criteria are used in the data collection process. Data may be classified based on time (indicates trends, rates of change, etc.), place, responsibility, structure, and influencing factors. The purpose of classification or categorization is to analyze results by groups, categories, or classes (cross-tabulation). Cross-tabulation allows the inspection of differences among groups to make comparisons. A common use of cross-tabulation is the separation of data into an experimental group and a control group to understand the effects of a treatment on one of the groups.

The technique for data analysis depends on the nature of the problem and the objectives of the assignment. One of the main objectives of analysis is to establish relationships between factors and events. Statistical techniques, such as regression, are commonly used to understand relationships. Multiple regression is a statistical technique that uses historical information on various factors and the performance measure that is studied and produces a mathematical function that shows the relationship of the various factors to the performance measure. It also helps understand the level of significance of the variable in its influence over the performance measure.

CHAPTER 11

Consulting Process— Solution Development

Solution development is the third phase in a typical consulting assignment. It is based on detailed, precise, and comprehensive analysis of the problem and its causes, plus the factors and forces that influence the change process in the client organization. While the emphasis in the previous phase was systematic and detailed analytical work, the emphasis in this phase is on innovation and creativity.

The client's involvement in the solution development phase is highly desirable since it:

1. generates commitment that is needed in the implementation phase;

2. provides a valuable learning opportunity to the client;

3. requires talent to generate and examine several ideas for solving the problem; the process can be enhanced if the client participates in the generation and evaluation of ideas; and

4. helps ascertain the feasibility of implementing the ideas.

In some consulting assignments, the consultant works independently in the development of solutions without the active involvement of the client since:

1. the client may lack resources to assist the consultant;

2. the client may be focused on other problems and expects the consultant to work independently;

3. the client may have developed a solution approach, but wants the consultant to develop a method independently so that it can be used to confirm the previously developed approach or to learn the process by which the consultant developed the approach; and

4. the client assumes that the consultant is obligated to develop the solution approach independently since the consultant is paid for that purpose.

11.1 Generation of Alternative Solutions

Solution development begins with a search for all possible solutions and ends with the selection of the best one. Most management problems have more than one, and in some cases many possible solutions. The consultant and client have a choice of searching for standard solutions (those that are readily available) or novel solutions. The following factors should be considered while searching for solutions:

1. nature of the problem;

2. technical aspects;

3. complexity (technical, financial, human, etc.); and

4. degree of familiarity with the problem.

A consultant uses knowledge gained from various sources in the generation of solutions. They include:

1. previous assignments conducted by the consultant;

2. reports on assignments conducted by other consultants in the firm;

3. assignments conducted by other consulting firms;

4. articles in professional journals; and

5. discussions with client staff about their experiences.

If a problem is similar to a previous assignment, the same solution may be applied. This is possible with problems that are of a progressive nature. Creative problems require innovative thinking. New ideas can be generated if the consultant and client are aware of barriers to creative thinking and how to break them. Creative thinking can be restricted due to any of the following reasons:

1. self-imposed barriers;

2. lack of effort in challenging the status quo;

3. belief that there is only one correct answer;

4. evaluating too quickly;

5. fear of looking unintelligent; and

6. respect and fear of authority.

One of the important creative thinking approaches is brainstorming, which obtains a large number of ideas from a group of people in a short period of time. During brainstorming, judgment is suspended and all types of ideas are encouraged. It is widely used and easy to administer.

11.2 Evaluation

If a large number of ideas are generated, they need to be reviewed, discussed, and assessed so as to produce a smaller set of ideas that will be subjected to a comprehensive evaluation. The following conditions are common in the evaluation of alternatives:

1. an alternative may not be the best in terms of all the criteria (i.e., an alternative may be the best in terms of cost and another alternative may be the best in terms of flexibility, but it is difficult to find an alternative that is the best in terms of both cost and flexibility);

2. positive and negative aspects of alternatives need to be compared;

3. number of criteria may be high;

4. specification of criteria and their importance is difficult; and

5. some criteria are difficult to quantify.

There are several techniques for organizing the information related to alternatives and preferences and to systematically conduct the evaluation. A simple method for evaluating alternatives is the scoring method. It helps organize and combine both quantitative and qualitative factors in the decision process. The steps include:

1. developing a list of alternatives and relevant criteria;

2. assigning a weight for each criterion;

3. assigning a score for each alternative;

4. multiplying the score and weight;

5. totalling the weighted scores for each alternative; and

6. selecting the alternative that has the highest score.

In the example below, alternative B is preferred because it has the highest score based on the criteria, their weights, and the scores for each alternative.

| Relevant Criteria | Weight | Alternative A | | Alternative B | |
		Score	Weighted Score	Score	Weighted Score
Production cost	0.5	80	$0.5 \times 80 = 40$	60	$0.5 \times 60 = 30$
Availability of labor	0.3	40	$0.3 \times 40 = 12$	80	$0.3 \times 80 = 24$
Markets	0.1	60	$0.1 \times 60 = 6$	50	$0.1 \times 50 = 5$
Environment	0.1	20	$0.1 \times 20 = 2$	60	$0.1 \times 60 = 6$
Total	**1.0**		**60**		**65**

11.3 Selection of Preferred Solution

The evaluation process leads to selection of a solution that is preferred over other solutions. The selection of a solution depends on the number of alternate solutions, number of decision-makers involved, and number of criteria used in the evaluation process and their complexity. The selection is trivial if a single decision-maker in the client organization is involved in evaluating a single solution recommended by the consultant based on a few criteria, such as cost and productivity. However, systematic methods are needed for selecting a preferred solution if there are several alternate solutions that need to be evaluated based on several criteria by a group of decision-makers. There are various methods, such as intuition, game theory, optimization, and decision analysis, that will assist the decision-makers in the discussion and help them to arrive at a consensus regarding the preferred solution.

A simple approach is to identify a desired solution that serves as a reference, compare all the alternate solutions to the desired solution, and select the solution that is closest to the desired solution. The following table shows the scores for the desired solution and for alternative solutions (higher score is preferred).

Relevant Criteria	Desired	Alt A	Alt B	Alt C	Alt D
Production cost	40	40	30	35	50
Availability of labor	20	12	24	18	4
Markets	5	6	5	3	10
Environment	5	2	6	3	2
Total	**70**	**60**	**65**	**59**	**66**

The difference between the desired solution and each of the alternate solutions can be shown in a tabular variation, as in the following table. Note that the difference is in absolute terms (i.e., the negative signs are dropped). The preferred solution in this example is alternative C, since it is close to the desired solution (11 is the least difference from the desired solution).

Relevant Criteria	Alt A	Alt B	Alt C	Alt D
Production cost	0	10	5	10
Availability of labor	8	4	2	16
Markets	1	0	2	5
Environment	3	1	2	3
Total	**12**	**15**	**11**	**34**

11.4 Presentation of Solution

In large and complex assignments, the consultant staff is involved in the generation and evaluation of solutions and keeps the senior management informed of the progress. Progress reports are submitted periodically so that the final reports do not present something unexpected. The information presented in the progress reports during solution development and earlier stages is summarized and presented in the final report for submission to the client. The objective of the presentation is to obtain the client's acceptance of the recommendations. Also included in the report is a macro-level description of how the solution will be implemented. The presentation includes a clear description of the evaluation techniques used, assumptions made, the risks involved, the changes that should be made to effectively implement the solution, and the forecasted costs needed for implementation.

CHAPTER 12

Consulting Process— Implementation

The basic purpose of many consulting assignments is to implement the changes proposed by the consultant and client team. Implementation is the fourth stage of the consulting process and can be considered the culmination of the collaborative work done by the consultant and client during the problem definition, data collection, diagnosis, and solution development stages.

The consultant may not be involved in the implementation if the following three conditions are met:

1. the problem and the solution are simple and can be easily implemented;

2. the client develops a very good understanding of the problem and solution during the joint work in the diagnostic and solution development phases; and

3. the client has the capability of implementing the proposed changes without the assistance of the consultant.

In addition, a client may not wish to involve the consultant in the implementation phase for financial reasons. The issue of the consultant's participation in the implementation phase should be examined and discussed during the proposal preparation stage.

12.1 Implementation Plan

The development of a detailed and sound implementation work plan is critical to a successful implementation phase. The implementation plan includes a definition of the tasks to be performed, when the tasks are to be performed, and who will perform them. This plan forms the basis for measuring the progress of the project. The important aspects of the implementation plan are:

1. *Scope*—To avoid confusion during the implementation, the boundaries of the implementation assignment should be clearly defined, that is, tasks that will be included in the implementation and those that will not be included.

2. *Tasks*—Identification and definition of all the tasks required to complete the installation. This refers to breaking down the implementation work into manageable units of work.

3. *Task times*—An estimate of the amount of time required to complete a task is developed based on guidelines or past experience with similar implementations.

4. *Resources*—After defining all the tasks, resources required to perform the task are identified. Certain tasks, such as supervision of the testing process, require experienced consultants, while some others may require less experienced staff. Also, implementation can result in new procedures and conditions in the client organization that involve new employees or existing employees in new roles. This requires training and development of the client personnel. Hence, one of the tasks of implementation would deal with training client personnel, which requires experienced consulting staff and other resources, such as equipment for training.

5. *Completion time*—The planned time for completion of implementation depends on the client's expectation and various technical and resource factors. The completion time may be specified in the contract or it may be decided before beginning the implementation. In addition to technical and resource factors, the time required for implementation depends on the commitment and support from the client's staff and the appropriate *pace of change* in the client's organization.

6. *Organizing the plan*—The plan is organized and documented using network methods such as PERT (Program Evaluation and Review Technique). These methods help to determine trade-offs between time and cost during implementation. Also, the methods help in the preparation of detailed reports by showing a list of tasks, their criticality, start and finish times of the tasks, resources required, and the sequence in which the tasks will be performed.

7. *Monitoring implementation*—A regular and frequent assessment of the progress of the implementation is made by the consultant and client. Monitoring helps in making appropriate adjustments to the times, schedules, tasks, and resources.

12.2 Training the Client's Staff

After implementation of the solution proposal by the consultant and conclusion of the assignment, the client operates in a changed environment. To be effective in the new environment, the client should have a clear understanding of the previous environment and the changes implemented by the consultant. This understanding is made possible through collaborative work with the consultant, supplemented by training.

Informal training takes place during the joint work performed by the consultant and the client. The client staff learns data collection procedures, observes and participates in the consultant's diagnosis and solution development procedures, and assists the consultant in implementing the solutions.

If a new technique is used in the assignment, such as statistical process control, individuals in the client's organization may be trained using formal training methods such as:

1. on-the-job training by the consultant;

2. training a few members who will train the remaining staff;

3. formal in-house training conducted by the consultant or external trainers; or

4. client personnel attendance at external training courses.

CHAPTER 13

Project Management—
Planning and Control

Project planning refers to the specification of objectives and evaluation criteria, and development of a framework for executing the assignment. Project control refers to the monitoring of progress of the various activities and changes to the schedules or resources to ensure timely completion of the assignment.

13.1 Project Planning

Project planning involves the specification of all the activities required to complete the assignment and related information. The plan outlines, in aggregate terms, the resources required for achieving the goals of the assignment. After the initial plan is developed, a more detailed schedule is prepared. The assignment is broken down into individual activities. The sequence of these activities is specified, and the time and resource requirements for each activity are estimated.

Network diagrams are commonly used for the planning and scheduling of assignments. A network diagram consists of a set of circles, called nodes, and a set of arrows, called arcs. The arcs connect the nodes and provide a visual presentation of the sequence in which activities will be executed. Activities that cannot be delayed are called critical activities, since they are important for timely completion of

44

the assignment. These activities receive the top priority in the alloca-
tion of resources and control efforts. Network-based methods also
help in estimating start and finish times of activities, slack time for
an activity (maximum amount of time by which the activity can be
delayed without delaying the assignment), expected completion time
of the assignment, and probability of completing the assignment in a
desired time period.

13.2 Project Control

The progress of various activities in the assignment is monitored
since the client is interested in the progress achieved for the fees paid
for the service. The consultant needs to use resources effectively so
that the assignment can be completed within time and budget constraints. Periodic reviews of the progress of the assignment are made
by the management of the consulting firm and the client organization. Assignments that are not on schedule and have technical, financial, and resource difficulties are subjected to a detailed discussion. If
the progress reports indicate a delay in activities compared to the
planned schedule, the consulting firm may increase the number of
operating consultants on critical activities. Also, the client staff could
increase their involvement and accelerate the critical activities. Time
required to complete the activities is not proportional to the number
of consultants added to the assignment. An increase in the number of
consultants requires additional effort for coordination and control.
Another approach for expediting the assignment is to subcontract a
portion of the assignment if it is clearly defined and structured (such
as implementation of a module in a management information system).

CHAPTER 14

Project Management— Documentation and Presentations

In addition to the proposal and final report, documentation includes all project findings, conclusions, time and costs, and other events during the project. They should be properly documented and filed by the consultant. Data collected during the project is recorded in documents or work papers. Documentation is done for various reasons:

1. as a historical substantiation of work performed;

2. as a source of reference for the consultant during the project;

3. to support the recommendations made by the consultant at the end of the project;

4. for administration purposes—time and amount of resources used helps in computing the fees that the client pays;

5. for maintaining a record of fee payment; and

6. for legal purposes.

14.1 Documentation

Work papers can be grouped into three categories:

1. *Administrative*—Work papers dealing with billing, time analysis, checklists, table of contents, references to other documents; these may be further grouped into indexes, checklists, and controls;

2. *Summary*—A brief description of proposals, interim and final reports, and any correspondence with the client; and

3. *Detail*—Detailed information such as interview results, questionnaire data, data on client operations, client reports, and research data on industry background, and data from similar client projects.

Some projects may require a standard format for recording information. Work papers should be organized in such a way that they can be easily retrieved. Indexes, section headers in the reports, table of contents, cross-references, etc. help to identify specific documents. Also, a standard format for cover pages helps in organizing the work papers (sample shown below).

Sample Format	
Client name	Client A
Client number	123-456
Project date	Jan 1, ... --Jun 30, ...
File number	DETAIL-RES-11
Index to other files	SUMM-RPT-1.1 DETL-RPT-2.1
Updates	John A. Doe / Jan 15, ... John B. Doe / Feb 16, ... John C. Doe / Apr 15, ...

Cross-referencing is used to link multiple documents. It reduces duplication and provides a way to track detailed information about a topic in the summary report. It is helpful to those who review documents in a long and complex project. Cross-referencing is accomplished through the use of a reference number for each document. Each document has this unique reference number and, in the document, the reference numbers of all other related documents may be mentioned. For example, detail on a special topic (marketing) in the final report may be obtained from a detailed report (survey result) using a reference number. A reference number in the detailed report (survey result) may be used to cross-reference another document (questionnaire data).

14.2 Other Documentation Issues

Effective management of large projects requires formal documentation policies. These policies for documentation should cover sample formats/standard structure, responsibilities, instructions, and timing for preparation, updating, and completion of documentation.

An explanation of these formats, examples showing how the formats can be used, and suggested formats for various parts of the project are helpful for documentation. Responsibilities for documentation should be assigned to the consultants at the beginning of the project. To ensure proper documentation, the consultants should use checklists and conduct periodic reviews of the documentation.

Based on the policies of the consulting firm and the requirements of the client, the documents should be retained for some period. Most organizations save the paper documents in a central file room and in other ways, such as microfiche, or in electronic storage medium, such as magnetic tapes.

14.3 Presentations

All consulting assignments culminate in a presentation of results to the client. Presentations involve two basic issues: what material to present and what method of presentation to use. Work papers collected during the project are summarized into important points and organized into a readable format. The type of presentation depends on the nature of the project, any contractual agreement or commitment, time and costs, etc. For example, the presentation for a training program may include lecture notes, videotapes, case studies, and visual aids. A classical method for presentation is the written report. It requires considerable time and effort and is less effective than an audiovisual presentation.

CHAPTER 15

Consulting Process—
Conclusion

Every consulting assignment is brought to an end when its purpose is achieved and the consultant's assistance is no longer needed. Conclusion of the consulting assignment is the last phase of the consulting process. It deals with two important aspects of the consulting process: the task for which the consultant is brought in and the consultant-client relationship.

Conclusion implies that the consultant is withdrawn from the project because the project is completed, discontinued, or will be pursued without the assistance of the consultant.

The manner in which the client-consultant relationship is terminated influences future assignments to the consultant. Since the last impressions are significant, a good performance at the end of the assignment and satisfactory financial closure leaves the door open for future projects. The client should be convinced that the assignment was successful and the consultant's assistance was valuable. The consultant should feel that the assignment provided a stimulating experience which was financially profitable and resulted in trust and respect from the client.

15.1 Timing of Withdrawal

Lack of proper planning may result in assignments that are terminated too early or too late. To avoid mishaps, the timing of withdrawal should be discussed at the beginning of the consulting process, and the consultant should clearly define the timing and conditions under which the conclusion will take place. An assignment may take longer than expected if the project is not clearly defined and new problems arise during the project or the client is not properly trained to take over from the consultant. It may be terminated too early if the client's budget does not permit the project to be completed, the consultant is in a hurry to start another project, or due to unexpected changes in the client's organization.

Conclusion may also occur at the end of the data collection and diagnosis phase or solution development phase, or at some stage of the implementation phase. At the time of signing the contract, it may be difficult to foresee how the project will progress, i.e., how the client will be involved and what problems may be discovered and, therefore, it is difficult to determine the right time for withdrawal. It is a good practice to specify critical termination evaluation points during the project when a review of the project's progress will be conducted to determine the remaining work to be accomplished. The consultant should also watch for withdrawal signals from the client. For example, a withdrawal signal from the client may indicate that the consultant has spent enough time on the project. The consultant should be alert to these signals and take necessary actions.

15.2 Evaluation by the Client

Evaluation of the consulting assignment is required to assess the benefits to the client and to check if the objectives of the client and consultant are met. Evaluation of the benefits involves a comparison of two situations, one before and one after the assignment. The benefits could be:

1. better performance in terms of productivity, financial status, or social performance of the client;

51

2. improved systems, with better procedures and information systems; and

3. greater capability, with new skills acquired by the client, such as diagnostic and problem-solving, communication, technical, and managerial skills.

Since the outcome of the assignment is dependent on the consulting style, an evaluation of the consulting style and intervention methods used during the project is useful. This evaluation involves the assessment of:

1. inputs provided by the consultant (size of the consultant team, skills, structure, and competence) and client (required information and time);

2. consulting style used (level of mutual trust, understanding, respect, and support);

3. project management (project monitoring and control, project management under changed conditions); and

4. contract preparation (Does the contract clearly describe the objectives, consulting style, inputs needed, roles and responsibilities of those involved, etc.?).

While evaluation may be done at various stages of the assignment, the end-of-assignment evaluation is the important one.

15.3 Follow-up

Follow-up refers to continued work on an assignment that is terminated. The need for follow-up is often identified during evaluation of the assignment. If a follow-up is in the client's interest, a suggestion is made by the client in the final report. New assignments may develop from the follow-up visits.

A follow-up arrangement is made only if the client feels the need for it, especially if the client desires assistance if new problems arise due to new technical developments. These follow-up visits are generally arranged for a short period of time following the end of the assignment. However, a relationship for an extended period of time

52

may be arranged with the consultant, called a "retainer arrangement" or "retainer contract." Under this contract, the consultant is available to the client for a specified amount of time every month or quarter, where the consultant may be working in an advisory role. The rules and job content are clearly defined in advance.

15.4 Final Report

Apart from the various interim reports, a final report is prepared and presented to the client at the end of the assignment. The final report should contain a comprehensive review of the work performed on the assignment, an evaluation of the benefits resulting from the assignment, recommendations to the client, and any need for follow-up work.

CHAPTER 16

Consultant Management—
Consulting Company
Business Plan

The purpose of a business plan is to provide a logical and rational sense of direction and to provide a framework for guiding and evaluating the consulting firm's achievements. A business plan is prepared to communicate the seriousness of the planning process and the framework for managing the firm, and to provide the lenders and investors with a sense of assurance that the firm can perform financially as mentioned in the plan. The basic information in the business plan includes organization and type of services, market analysis, and revenue projections.

The internal uses of the plan are:

1. to identify strengths and weaknesses of the firm and help build on the strengths and correct the weaknesses;

2. to coordinate and ensure consistency in the plans of various units if multiple units are present;

3. to communicate to consultants and administrative staff the firm's performance expectations and priorities; and

4. to establish a standard for performance evaluation.

The external uses are:

1. to communicate to outside parties (financial and regulatory bodies) the objectives, structure, and performance of the firm; and

2. to obtain funding from outside investors.

16.1 Strategies and Objectives

The basic question in defining consulting strategies is "Why should a client come to us rather than to other consultants?" The answer may be due to special technical expertise, knowledge in an industrial sector, low fees, good reputation, etc. It is essential to possess a competitive advantage or to develop one. The consulting firm needs to define its purpose and objectives from a professional and organizational point of view. From a professional point of view, it should address the following:

1. What kind of professional firm should it be?

2. What type of leadership should it have?

3. What type of professional services should it offer?

4. What type of professional culture and consulting philosophy should it possess?

From an organizational point of view, it should address the following:

1. What growth rate should it have?

2. What earnings should be achieved?

3. What is the optimum size of the firm?

16.2 Organizing the Practice

Like any business, the consulting business needs to arrange resources (financial, human, equipment, and facilities) and identify the client base. Market analysis helps in defining the client base. The important factors for defining the client base include:

1. type of organization (large, medium, or small);

2. type of sector (banking, transportation, or health care);

3. private, public, or nonprofit organization;

4. number of clients; and

5. location of clients.

The client base, planned growth rate, and types of services help determine the resources needed over time. The number and type of consultants, administrative staff, facilities, and equipment require financing, which may be invested by the consultant or by lenders and investors. Capital is needed to obtain resources and pay basic operating expenses, such as salaries, rent, office supplies, etc. The firm may be established as a sole proprietorship, partnership, or corporation. The legal form depends on factors such as legal liability, income tax issues, and personal objectives. Revenue projections are based on the number and type of assignments to be managed and the fees. A simple projection for a sole practitioner for a year may be computed as: 2,000 hours per year deducted from 800 hours per year (for holidays, vacation, administrative, training, etc.) = 1,200 hours per year × $80 revenue per hour = $96,000 per year.

16.3 Building the Firm

The consulting firm generally starts with one or more clients. The early growth of the consulting practice depends largely on the success of initial client assignments and marketing efforts. An effective implementation of the marketing plan, an awareness of the competition, and an appropriate adjustment to competition and changes in the environment help in building the consulting practice.

16.4 Monitoring Results

A framework is needed to monitor the financial and operational performance of the consulting firm in order to share profits with the employees and to remain competitive in the marketplace. Performance is generally assessed by:

1. Comparing results against planned targets helps to identify any weakness in performance or error in setting the targets. In either case, appropriate action is taken to correct any weakness.

2. Comparing results with past performance helps with the discovery and analysis of trends and the factors influencing them.

3. Comparing results with other consulting firms helps to identify weaknesses in operations, unforeseen changes in the environment, etc.

Performance results may be produced at various levels, such as type of service, region, department, and consultant. They should be reviewed and corrective action taken on a regular basis. The performance results, corrective actions or changes in priorities, and the desired results should be communicated to the consultants.

CHAPTER 17

Consultant Management— Marketing Consulting Services

Marketing is essential for management consultants to remain competitive and to make the right consultants available to the client who needs them. Marketing for management consulting firms involves self-assessment, assessment of the marketing for consulting services, review of techniques for marketing the service, information for marketing, and an audit of marketing practices.

17.1 Self-Assessment

Self-assessment refers to obtaining a realistic view of how the consulting firm is perceived by the external environment (image), its resources and capabilities (profile), and its past performance in terms of successes and failures (position).

The perception of the existing and potential clients about the consultant (image) may be fully consistent with the consultant's real capabilities and performance record. However, for a variety of reasons, there may be a difference between the image and the real capabilities. These include:

1. excessive publicity given by the media to a poorly executed project;

2. unsuccessful advertising and promotion effort; and

58

3. poor assessment of the image.

The most important resources of a consulting firm are the human resources. Self-assessment should include a careful examination of each employee's background in terms of education, technical skills, management and consulting experience, work capacity, age and positions, motivation and entrepreneurial spirit, flexibility and adaptability to new tasks and situations, and potential for further development.

The consulting firm's growth rate, contributions to the client's performance, innovations in methods and products, improvements in professional standards, achievements in mobilizing resources and effectiveness in utilizing them, and any other developments must be examined.

17.2 Market Assessment

Assessment of the market for consulting services involves existing clients, potential clients, and other related factors in the external environment.

Since the relationship with the existing client has a major impact on the opportunity for additional assignments for the client and on the image of the consulting firm, an examination is needed in areas such as:

1. consultant-client relationship;

2. fit between the client's needs and the consultant's capabilities; and

3. client's intent in offering more assignments to the consultant.

The task of identifying and assessing potential clients is undertaken by new consulting firms as well as existing consulting firms. This task requires considerable research using extensive information and research methods. The research may result in a large set of potential clients or a smaller set of organizations that have an immediate need for consulting services. Market segmentation is helpful in dividing the large set of potential clients into smaller sets based on a variety of criteria, such as size, location, markets served, type of products, or nature and severity of difficulties.

An assessment of the market should also focus on other factors that influence management consulting, such as government policies, political climate, business community, local culture and traditions, availability, and sources of finance for development projects.

17.3 Techniques

A variety of techniques are available to a consulting firm for its marketing efforts. Based on the purpose, marketing techniques can be grouped into those that are aimed at building an image or positioning the consulting firm and those that are meant to find clients and offer services for specific projects.

Techniques for marketing the consulting firm attempt to project the image of a professional and capable organization. Some of the important techniques are described below.

Advertising arouses the interest of potential clients by providing information and attempting to convince them that the consulting services are suitable to tackle their performance problems. Essential information that emphasizes the benefits that a client expects should be included.

The media for the advertisements should be carefully selected. They include:

1. journals and newspapers that the potential clients are likely to read;

2. radio and television during special programs that are aimed at businesses;

3. direct mailings that include company reports;

4. information brochures;

5. reprints of articles from journals;

6. profiles of consulting staff;

7. exhibitions at trade fairs and professional conventions; and

8. videotapes sent to prospective clients.

Addresses for potential clients may be obtained from trade associations or professional associations.

Management seminars, workshops, conferences, and similar events on a topic of interest to the client and on topics that are the consultant's expertise are a popular way of attracting clients and demonstrating to them that the consulting firm is up-to-date on the subject matter and is eager to assist the client in solving their problem and improving their performance. Generally, these events include presentations by invited speakers who are experts in the subject matter (such as scientists, professors, leading managers, CEOs) in addition to a presentation by the staff of the consulting firm.

Directories provide a listing of management consultants with the contact name and addresses followed by a brief description of the types of services offered. This is an economical way of reaching potential clients.

Referral is the most effective way in which a consultant gets in contact with new clients. A manager in a client organization who needs consulting assistance is likely to seek advice from professional colleagues. Any referral that the manager gets would be most likely about a consultant who provided an excellent service to the client. Hence, to get good referrals, the consultant should ensure that clients are happy with the service and also discuss promotional needs with them. The consultant should request authorization to use the client's name as a reference to potential clients, request permission to use a summary of a successful assignment in a journal or promotional material, and request assistance in the promotional activities. Satisfied clients are the best marketers for the consulting firm.

Publications are another effective way to market a consulting service. The consulting firm may prepare and distribute a newsletter that contains articles devoted to a specific industry or a topic on a periodical basis. A professionally produced newsletter may become a highly regarded service that provides valuable information to the clients, both existing and potential ones. If publications cannot be produced on a periodical basis, occasional pamphlets briefly describing the consultant's experience in successful projects and any state-of-the-art information would be an attractive way to provide clients with useful information and to enhance the client's image. Also, books published by the consulting staff have a strong impact on promoting new business. Since writing a book is a difficult and time-consuming exercise, and managers in the client organizations may not read the book unless it is highly recommended, an easier approach is publication of shorter articles in professional, business, and trade journals that are read by more people.

The use of the *Internet* as a medium is yet another effective and economical approach for providing information to potential clients. Information about the consulting firm may be:

1. sent to potential clients via e-mail;

2. presented at a web site that can be accessed by clients; and

3. linked to web sites of professional and trade organizations.

Marketing for specific consulting services may be done using the following techniques.

Cold contacts include telephone calls, letters, and visits by a consultant to a potential client with the objective of selling a service. A cold contact is generally initiated by a letter that is not detailed or vague but shows that the consultant has something specific and relevant to offer. It is followed by a telephone call requesting an appointment, and then a visit to the client.

Contacts based on referrals may involve a consultant obtaining the names of potential clients from a business friend, a consultant obtaining names of potential clients from the current client, or a prospective client approaching the consultant. A good referral creates a favorable atmosphere for an informative discussion and a good possibility of obtaining an assignment.

Invitations for proposals involve a published notice in a newspaper or periodical inviting consultants to present a proposal for a project. This involves a standard procedure for submitting proposals. In the first step, all interested consulting firms submit a preliminary proposal indicating their interest and information about their firm. The client then prepares a short list of consultants and invites them to submit detailed proposals that are examined and selected by the client.

17.4 Information for Marketing

Any effort for marketing consulting services requires information on various areas:

1. *Clients*—Names and addresses of the client, contact persons in the client organizations, past and current projects, and other consulting firms that worked for the client.

2. *Markets*—The industry, competitors, change in the markets, any developments, impact of government policies, etc.

3. *Internal*—Past and current marketing efforts by the consulting firm. Names and activities of all persons involved in marketing, their achievements, qualitative and quantitative information on these topics so that the firm may audit its marketing efforts. Information on qualitative factors such as personality and capability of consultants should be available in the information system so that members of the consulting firm who have the best marketing potential could be assigned to various marketing activities.

17.5 Marketing Audit

Marketing audit refers to an assessment of a consulting firm's past marketing practices. The purpose of the audit is to recommend measures for making the marketing activities more effective. It involves:

1. examination of the marketing strategy, techniques, information, pricing strategies, etc. and an assessment of their impact on the firm;

2. examination of competitors' marketing practices and a comparison with them; and

3. development of new plans to meet the requirements of the market and the consulting firm's objectives.

CHAPTER 18

Consultant Management—
Finance

Like any organization, a consulting firm has to manage the costs of operating the firm and income obtained from fees charged to the client for its products and services. Before an assignment can begin, the consultant estimates the cost of the assignment and uses it in the negotiation and preparation of the contract. The fee that is charged to a client is a function of the cost of service, income that the consultant expects to earn, appropriateness of the fee in a market, and the ability and willingness of a client to pay it. Estimates of costs and income form the basis for building a budget for the consulting firm.

18.1 Costs

A consulting firm incurs a variety of costs (shown in the table on the following page). Since management consulting is highly labor-intensive, the primary costs are salary and benefits paid to the consultants, administrators, and support staff. In a typical firm, salaries constitute about two-thirds of the total costs, while other costs are about one-third.

TYPES OF COSTS

Salaries
    – Consultants
    – Management
    – Support

Facility rent and utilities
Equipment, furniture, and stationery
Depreciation and amortization
Communications (mail, fax, phone, etc.)
Library, subscriptions, membership fees
Training, travel, and entertainment
Interest and taxes

Direct labor cost is the amount of time required to carry out the assignment times the cost per unit time. A correct assessment of time for the assignment requires considerable experience and preparation of a detailed work plan. This assessment is typically performed by senior consultants. In a new assignment there may be a precise plan for the initial phases, but only a rough assessment for the later stages. In such cases both the client and consultant may be unclear about the time and volume of work required and may prefer to use a phased approach where time and cost are assessed at specified stages during the project. The time unit used for calculating costs is typically an hour or day.

Nondirect labor cost generally includes the salaries and benefits for administrative, technical, clerical, supervisory, and other support staff.

Other costs for travel, food and hotel, communications, photocopying, etc. are either included in the fee that is charged to the client or considered to be "billable" or "reimbursable" costs that are not a part of the fee but are submitted separately to the client for reimbursement.

Overhead includes a variety of costs related to facility rent, utilities, equipment, library, nondirect labor costs, etc. Overhead cost refers to all the expenses that cannot be assigned to a specific consulting assignment.

Cost estimate of a consulting assignment is the sum of direct labor, and any assignment-specific costs such as travel, and overhead costs.

Assuming a consultant's average salary is $80,000 per year, the number of fee-earning days in a year is 200 and work hours are 8 hours a day, the cost per hour is [$80,000 / (8 × 200)] = $50, and the cost per day = $80,000 / 200 = $400. The unit costs vary by the experience of the consultants and the area of specialization. If different types of consultants are used in an assignment, the direct labor cost is computed using the time and unit cost for each type of consultant used.

Suppose the consulting firm has 100 consultants and incurs $4,000,000 per year for overhead expenses. Allocating the overhead expenses among all the consultants equally results in $40,000 per consultant per year or [$40,000 / (8 × 200)] = $25 per hour or $40,000 / 200 = $200 per day. The cost estimate for the assignment would be the sum of direct labor cost and overhead cost ($50 + $25 = $75 per hour).

18.2 Fees

A consulting firm charges a fee for most of its services. However, certain services, such as short surveys and research done for preparing a proposal, may not be charged. Also, services such as management seminars and work toward publication of material for potential clients are free and are considered a part of the marketing effort.

Methods for fee setting vary; the important ones are described below.

Flat fee: With this type of method, a client pays a flat (lump-sum) fee to the consultant if the project is completed according to the terms and conditions of the consulting contract. Examples of consulting assignments that have a flat-fee include market surveys, feasibility studies, design of a plant layout, etc. A flat fee is attractive only for projects that are clearly defined. The consultant benefits if the project actually takes less time than the specified time in the contract.

Time-based fee: With this method, the fee that a client pays is the amount of time spent on the project times the fee per unit of time specified in the contract. For example, if an assignment is completed in 100 hours and the fee is $80 per hour, the fee paid by the client is 100 hours × $80 per hour = $8,000.

Different types of consultants have different fees per unit time; senior consultants have a higher fee. This method is simple and easy to manage. A client pays the fee on a periodical basis (once a month or once a week) based on the time spent by the consultant on the project. A disadvantage with this method is that some clients may feel that the consultants try to prolong the assignment. Any misunderstanding can be avoided if the duration of the project is clearly defined in the contract and there is an atmosphere of trust in the consultant's integrity and competence.

Results-based fee: With this method, the fee is based on achievement of the results and magnitude of the results. The consultant is paid only if the client assignment shows results. The advantage of this method is the focus on achieving bottom-line results rather than in the preparation of reports and research work. The disadvantages of this method include focus on short-term results and neglect of activities that may result in long-term benefits, difficulties in measuring results, and factors not related to the consultant's effort that may not produce results (such as strikes, weather, or poor economy).

Hybrid methods: Some methods may be a combination of the three methods discussed above. A hybrid method may involve the client paying a time-based fee up to an upper limit on the time, after which a flat fee is paid. For example, suppose the duration of the project specified in the contract is 100 hours. The client may agree to pay $50 per hour, to a maximum of $5,000 for the project. If the project completes in 80 hours, the client pays $4,000 and if the project takes 150 hours, the client pays only $5,000.

Fee-related aspects: Payment schedule refers to an arrangement where a client pays the consultant according to the schedule. A common schedule is periodical—the client pays once a month or once a week.

The fees, methods for calculating the fees, and payment schedules should be communicated to the client in the initial stage of the assignment. In some cases, they may be negotiated. The client may request details about time for the assignment and the estimation of the fee. The consultant should be prepared to provide the justification of the proposed time and fees for the assignment. Negotiation may involve reducing the time required and reducing the fees by using a different mix of consulting staff.

18.3 Budgets

Budgets include all the costs that the consulting firm expects to incur during the budget period and the income required to recover the costs and make a desired profit. The budget is based on an operating work plan that shows:

1. expected volume of consulting and other services during the budget period;

2. expected workforce levels, recruitment, and training;

3. mix of consulting assignments; and

4. volume and type of marketing activities.

If the budget is not satisfactory, the work plan and assumptions made in the cost and fee-setting methods are revised. The budget is prepared so that a desired level of profit may be obtained. Typically, a profit margin of 10–25% of total income is expected. This profit is used for paying taxes; profit-sharing or bonuses to the owners, partners, and employees of the firm; salaries; and for expanding the operation. Following are some of the methods used to increase profits:

1. Increase consulting fees

2. Reduce free services

3. Reduce overhead expenses

4. Execute assignments efficiently

5. Enhance marketing activities

6. Recruit better and more consulting staff

7. Provide new types of services

8. Develop an optimal mix of services

CHAPTER 19

Consultant Management— Assignment Management

Management of consulting organizations involves two aspects: management of the consulting organization and management of the consulting assignments. The main part of the consultant's work is assignments in the client organization. After a proposal is made and the client and consultant agree and sign a contract, a self-contained management team is formed in the consulting firm. After the assignment is completed, these teams cease to exist and the consultants are assigned to another team for a different assignment. During the assignment, the working time and expertise of the consultants belong to the client. The team leader must be able to manage the resources to deliver the service.

19.1 Planning the Assignment

The assignment plan includes the main activities shown on a timetable (weeks or days), start and finish times of the activities, volume of work in each period (mandays), and points of time when reports will be submitted. A short assignment is generally planned in greater detail than a longer assignment.

A key person in the management of assignments is the team leader or project manager. Typically, senior consultants with considerable experience and achievements are given this role. They are generally involved in conducting the preliminary analysis for submitting the proposal and negotiating the contract. After the contract is signed and the assignment begins, the team leader has responsibilities such as work scheduling, guidance to the operating consultants, review of important reports and proposals to be submitted to the client, and control and assessment of progress.

19.2 Managing Assignment Execution

Management consulting involves decentralization of decision making and control. Most decisions and control of assignments rest with the consulting team working on the assignment. Generally, decisions for most problems are decided on the spot by the consultant or the team leader.

Assignment execution depends on the performance of the supervisor and the operating consultants and their relationship with the client. The supervisor visits the client as frequently as needed and checks if the client is satisfied with:

1. the overall progress of the assignment;

2. contributions made by the operating consultants; and

3. relationships between the client and the operating consultants.

The supervisor also discusses the assignment and progress with the operating consultants and provides guidance. The supervisor checks the following activities of the operating consultants:

1. assignment progress is up-to-date and under control;

2. proper documentation is maintained;

3. frequent and satisfactory contacts are made with the client; and

4. morale and enthusiasm are high.

Every organization has unique behavioral patterns, habits, and traditions. The operating consultant should decide how to operate in this environment and set an example for effective work and intellectual integrity. The consultant is likely to encounter frustrations and must endure them with patience and good humor. The consultant should adjust to the working hours of the client organization. An assignment diary should be maintained by the supervisor and all significant events and progress should be recorded in it.

19.3 Records

An accurate and reliable system of records and reports is needed for effective management of the assignment, charging clients properly, and paying the consultants their salaries and reimbursing their expenses. Apart from reports related to the findings and recommendations, the team leader prepares survey notes about the client organization and an assignment summary. An assignment summary consists of information on:

1. the client's name and address;

2. names and titles of client staff involved in the project;

3. nature and size of the organization;

4. names of the consulting team member;

5. start and end date of the assignment;

6. an index of all reports; and

7. a brief summary of the objectives and results.

Important records for bookkeeping and administration are the consultant's time records and receipts of expenses incurred by the consultant. A consultant time record shows the following information: name of the consultant, period of work, names of clients interacted with, fee rates for paid work, number of fee-earning days, number of nonfee-earning days (showing sick days, training, promotional activity, etc.). This is helpful in computing salaries for the consultant and keeping track of the number of vacation days, sick days, and other personnel-related information. Proper reimbursement of expenses is possible if the receipts for expenses are saved. Receipts for important items are provided to the client so that they are available for tax purposes and auditing.

CHAPTER 20

Consultant Management— Consultant Development

Consultant development includes initial training to new employees, on-going training, and career development. A new employee in a consulting firm needs to acquire consulting skills, understand unique aspects of the consulting business, and understand the consulting firm's approach and philosophy. Though a new employee may have excellent educational background and experience, initial training is needed since:

1. consulting on how to do a job is different from actually doing the job;

2. the consulting firm may have a unique consulting philosophy and strategy, including consulting methods and techniques, ethics, objectives, etc.; and

3. the breadth and depth of knowledge required to work on a consulting assignment generally exceeds that of a new employee.

20.1 Initial Training

The initial training programs for new consultants varies from informal and unstructured to formal and structured programs, depending on the needs of the new consultants and the resources available in the consulting firm. A typical initial training program has the following components:

1. *training courses*—These deal with topics that are common to all consultants and may be covered in a few days. This may be followed by a presentation of specific problems and methods used by the consulting firm.

2. *practical field training*—This involves providing first-hand experience in consulting at work and develops a variety of practical skills. This type of training depends on the willingness of the client to receive trainees and the availability of senior consultants to provide training.

3. *independent study*—This includes independent reading of proposals, final assignment reports, manuals, and professional books for familiarity with the consulting firm's prior work and to bridge any gaps in technical skills.

The overall length of the initial training programs varies from firm to firm. However, the program should be thorough enough to demonstrate that the job is demanding in time, effort, and intellectual work, so that the consultant is clear about the responsibilities.

20.2 On-Going Training

Continued training is necessary to upgrade the competence of the consultants. Training may be done in one or more of the following areas:

1. *Acquiring new skills*—A consultant may learn topics other than his/her expertise for a variety of reasons (to become a generalist, to become active in new fields, or the consulting firm rotates its employees to new fields instead of hiring new consultants).

2. *Enhancing technical skills*—A consultant may enhance the skills by learning topics related to the field, including advanced material and latest developments.

3. *Enhancing other skills*—A new consultant may have adequate technical skills and knowledge about the consulting process

from the initial training. However, additional training that deals with the consultant-client relationship, methods for managing change in the client organization, etc. is needed to become an effective consultant.

While the initial training program may be structured, there may be no formal programs for on-going training. Consultants learn mostly from their own experience and that of the other consultants. This learning is generally supplemented by other opportunities:

1. *Guidance from senior consultants*—A senior consultant responsible for supervising an assignment provides guidance to the consultants on approaches to solving problems, communicating with the client, handling delicate matters, etc. Also, a consultant learns from discussions with the supervisor and other consultants working on an assignment.

2. *Training*—A consultant can enhance his/her presentation skills and knowledge on technical aspects if s/he is involved in training others (client's staff or other consultants).

3. *Reading*—This is a very common method of on-going training. Reading professional periodicals, technical articles, internal consulting reports, and other consulting industry-specific periodicals enhance the knowledge and skills of the consultant.

4. *Conferences*—Participation in conferences and seminars organized by the consulting firm or professional organizations is beneficial to the consultant. These help the consultant to learn new material and also help in the marketing effort.

5. *Other*—Activities dealing with the development of new services or products, preparing manuals based on prior assignments, and preparing budgets for the consulting firm are also excellent learning opportunities.

20.3 Career Development

A sole practitioner is a single-person consulting firm and has no one to promote him/her to a senior position. However, a sole practitioner may join a larger consulting firm in a senior position. Typically, consultants in senior positions have more responsibility. Negotiation with potential clients and management of assignments are generally done by the senior consultants. Consultants in junior positions are encouraged to assume responsibility for difficult tasks and supervision of these tasks.

Career advancement should be based on achievements; junior consultants should be treated as potential partners. A career development plan, based primarily on achievements rather than the period of time spent in the consulting firm, has a positive motivational effect and creates a dynamic and competitive environment.

CHAPTER 21

Consultant Management— Ethical and Legal Aspects

There is a wide variety of consulting organizations, and each is established using different legal organization forms. Tasks such as taxation, record keeping, and reporting depend on the legal form used for the consulting organization. A large international consulting firm may have to use different legal forms in the countries that it operates. Like other professions, consulting has a set of ethical norms that define what is appropriate and what is inappropriate behavior in providing consulting services.

21.1 Legal Aspects

Some management consulting units operate as divisions in organizations that have a wider scope of business (a management consulting division in an accounting firm or university). In such a case, the legal entity is not the management consulting unit but the organization in which it operates. There are three basic legal forms for management consulting firms that operate as independent units.

1. *Sole proprietorship*—A single person owns and operates the consulting business. Typically, this form is used by sole practitioners and small consulting firms. This is a simple form suitable for those who are starting in consulting and who prefer to remain completely independent in their career. The

net income of the firm is taxed as the owner's personal income and the owner is liable for all debts incurred by the firm. There is a high amount of risk in an operation of this type of firm in case of a prolonged illness of the owner. The firm normally ceases to exist with the death of the owner.

2. *Partnership*—This involves an agreement between two or more people to establish a firm by combining their skills and resources. They share all profits, losses, and liabilities based on the proportion agreed to in the contract. This is a common legal form used to set up small- and medium-size consulting firms. This helps in the effective utilization of facilities and technical skills and makes it possible to handle large and complex assignments. This type of firm can operate smoothly in the absence of a partner. However, this type of firm is not suitable if the partners cannot work together and do not trust each other. Disadvantages include unlimited liability for all partners for any errors committed by other partners and the need for a collective decision on all important issues.

3. *Corporation*—This is a legal entity in which the owners have no personal liability for the debts and obligations of the corporation. It offers considerable flexibility in conducting and developing the business—individuals can be owners and employees of the corporation, earnings can be retained for investment in the firm, and taxation is separate from personal income. This type of firm is required to comply with various reporting, auditing, and other rules. In some consulting firms that operate as corporations, the ownership is reserved to a group of senior consultants (officers, partners, principals) with a limit on the number of shares that can be owned by a single member.

21.2 Ethical Aspects

There are a number of professional associations in a number of countries that represent the interests of management consultants and regulate the activities of individual consultants and consulting firms. These associations play an important role in promoting professional standards of consulting and provide various services to its members. They attach a great deal of importance to professional ethics to protect integrity and inform clients about the standards and rules observed by the consultants. Following is a summary of the code of ethics specified by various professional associations:

1. The client's interests should be placed ahead of the consultants;

2. Serve the client with integrity, competence, and independence;

3. Advice to the client based on impartial consideration of all related facts;

4. All the client's information should be treated confidentially;

5. The client should be informed of any circumstance that might influence the judgment or objectivity of the consultant's services;

6. A consultant should take assignments for which s/he has required qualifications;

7. A consultant should not take an assignment for which effective service cannot be provided; and

8. Reasonable fees will be charged to the client which are agreed upon in the contract.

CHAPTER 22

Companies and Careers in Management Consulting

Almost every firm in the Fortune 500 list of firms has received assistance from management consulting firms. *Consulting News*, a consulting industry publication, estimates that about 250,000 people are employed in management consulting worldwide. One of the reasons that a client organization hires consultants is that it is more economical to outsource than to maintain a staff to work on such assignments. However, the fees paid to a typical consulting firm tend to be high enough that consultants get high salaries. High salaries, prestige of the consulting jobs, and the opportunity to learn and work on challenging problems attract some of the brightest people to consulting firms.

22.1 Consulting Jobs

Jobs in a typical consulting company may be grouped into five categories.

1. *Training/Internship*—These jobs involve assisting the consultants with data collection and documentation, and acquiring basic consulting skills. New consultants spend about six months in training and interns may spend a summer term as part of their university degree program.

2. *Consultant*—Consultant is the front-line employee who does a major part of the assignment in the client organization. Each consultant has a specialized expertise. A person with an M.B.A. degree or a graduate degree in a specialized subject, such as communications, joins the consulting firm in this position.

3. *Senior Consultant*—In addition to working on an assignment, a senior consultant is responsible for supervision of other consultants, marketing new assignments, interacting with the client staff, and providing progress reports.

4. *Principal/Senior Manager*—These consultants are responsible for middle-management and marketing functions. They coordinate and control several assignments, plan and negotiate new assignments, prepare budgets, and may serve as head of a department or group.

5. *Partner/Vice President/President*—They are concerned with developing the consulting practice, promotional work with key clients, managing large assignments, and participating in the strategy formulation for the firm.

22.2 List of Companies

A list of major management consulting firms is provided in the table on the following pages. For a detailed list of companies, the reader should refer to a directory of management consulting firms or the local telephone yellow pages.

Detailed information of the major management consulting companies may be obtained by contacting them at the addresses provided in the first column of the table. The third column shows a list of job positions at the company and the arrow indicates junior positions to senior positions.

There is also a column to give you a sense of the type of candidate. A fourth column is included to indicate the schools most commonly chosen for recruits. Also, it is generally agreed upon by consulting groups that a graduate degree is essential to the process of moving up and succeeding within a company.

22.3 Select Companies

Company	Number of Employees	Roles	Candidate Personality	Typical Candidate Education
Anderson Consulting 1345 Avenue of the Americas 8th Floor New York, NY 10105 Tel: (212) 708-4400 Web: http://www.ac.com	44,000	Partner Associate Partner Manager Consultant Analyst ←	• self-motivated • problem solver • successful track record	Harvard Business School Tuck MIT-Sloan Wharton Others welcome
Arthur D. Little, Inc. 25 Acorn Park Cambridge, MA 02140 Tel: (617) 498-5000 Web: http://www.arthurdlittle.com	1,272	Director Associate Director Senior Manager Manager Consultant Analyst ←	• interpersonal skills • analytical • forward-thinking • confident	Top business schools in U.S.
A.T. Kearney, Inc. 222 West Adams Street Chicago, IL 60606 Tel: (312) 648-0111 Web: http://www.atkearney.com	2,300	Officer Principal Manager Associate Business Analyst ←	• good communication skills • flexible • significant industry experience	Leading business schools in world
Bain and Company, Inc. Two Copley Place Boston, MA 02116 Tel: (617) 572-2000 Web: http://www.bain.com	1,350	Director Vice President Manager Consultant Associate Consultant ←	• team-centered • forward-thinking	Leading business schools
Booz Allen and Hamilton, Inc. 101 Park Avenue New York, NY 10178 Tel: (212) 697-1900 Web: http://www.bah.com	5,685	Vice President Principal Senior Associate Associate Consultant ←	• mature • analytical • experience preferred	Top eight MBA business schools
The Boston Consulting Group, Inc., 31st Floor Exchange Place, 53 State Street Boston, MA 02109 Tel: (617) 973-1200 Web: http://www.bcg.com	1,550	Officer Manager Case Leader Consultant Associate ←	• leadership • persuasive • energetic	Leading business schools
CSC Index Five Cambridge Center Cambridge, MA 02142-1493 Tel: (617) 520-1500 Web: http://www.csc.com	600	Partner Principal Managing Associate Associate Analyst ←	• strong academics • extra-curricular activity • four years prior experience	Berkeley Columbia Harvard Business School Fuqua Others welcome

22.3 Select Companies (continued)

Company	Number of Employees	Roles	Candidate Personality	Typical Candidate Education
Decision Focus, Inc. 650 Castro Street, Suite 300 Mountain View, CA 94041 Tel: (415) 960-2600 Web: http://www.dfi.com	150	Principal Senior Associate Associate II Associate I Analyst	• analytical • knowledge in areas of management science, software development, and business process development	Engineering schools: Stanford, Cornell, MIT, and Berkeley Business schools: Harvard and MIT
Deloitte and Touche Consulting Group 10 West Port Road P.O. Box 820 Wilton, CT 06897 Tel: (203) 761-3000 Web: http://www.dttus.com	8,857	Partner Senior Manager Manager Senior Consultant Consultant Analyst	• a quick mind • common sense minded • self-confident	Top MBA programs
Gemini Consulting 25 Airport Road Morristown, NJ 07960 Tel: (973) 285-9000 Web: http://www.gemcom.com	1,550	Senior Vice President Vice President Principal Manager Consultant Senior Consultant Consultant	• individuality • high tolerance of change and travel	Universities and Industry
McKinsey and Company, Inc. 55 East 52nd Street New York, NY 10022 Tel: (212) 446-7000 Web: http://www.mckinsey.com	3,944	Director (Sr. Partner) Principal (Partner) Associate Business Analyst	• capacity for continuous growth • work collaboratively	Variety of schools
Mercer Management Consulting, Inc. 1166 Avenue of the Americas New York, NY 10036 Tel: (212) 345-8000 Web: http://www.mercermc.com	9,241	Director Vice President Principal Senior Associate Business Analyst	• logical • team-oriented • curious	Top MBA business programs
Monitor Company 2 Canal Street Cambridge, MA 02141 Tel: (617) 252-2000 Web: http://www.monitor.com	700	Director Consultant	• keen intellect • interpersonal skills • competitiveness	World's top business schools
ZS Associates 1800 Sherman Avenue, Suite 700 Evanston, IL 60201 Tel: (847) 492-3409 Web: http://www.zsassociates.com	270	Principal Manager Consultant	• high energy • problem solver • creative	Harvard, Stanford, Kellogg, Darden, Sloan, Chicago, Warton, and Michigan

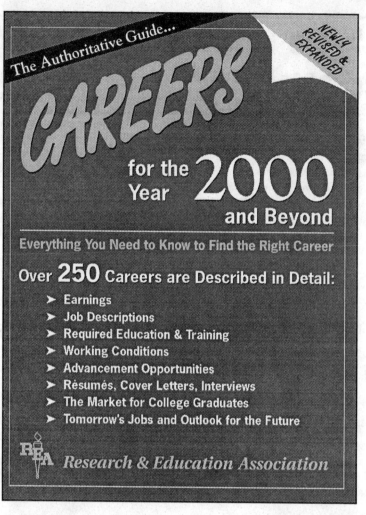

REA's **Problem Solvers**

The "PROBLEM SOLVERS" are comprehensive supplemental textbooks designed to save time in finding solutions to problems. Each "PROBLEM SOLVER" is the first of its kind ever produced in its field. It is the product of a massive effort to illustrate almost any imaginable problem in exceptional depth, detail, and clarity. Each problem is worked out in detail with a step-by-step solution, and the problems are arranged in order of complexity from elementary to advanced. Each book is fully indexed for locating problems rapidly.

ACCOUNTING
ADVANCED CALCULUS
ALGEBRA & TRIGONOMETRY
AUTOMATIC CONTROL
   SYSTEMS/ROBOTICS
BIOLOGY
BUSINESS, ACCOUNTING, & FINANCE
CALCULUS
CHEMISTRY
COMPLEX VARIABLES
DIFFERENTIAL EQUATIONS
ECONOMICS
ELECTRICAL MACHINES
ELECTRIC CIRCUITS
ELECTROMAGNETICS
ELECTRONIC COMMUNICATIONS
ELECTRONICS
FINITE & DISCRETE MATH
FLUID MECHANICS/DYNAMICS
GENETICS
GEOMETRY
HEAT TRANSFER

LINEAR ALGEBRA
MACHINE DESIGN
MATHEMATICS for ENGINEERS
MECHANICS
NUMERICAL ANALYSIS
OPERATIONS RESEARCH
OPTICS
ORGANIC CHEMISTRY
PHYSICAL CHEMISTRY
PHYSICS
PRE-CALCULUS
PROBABILITY
PSYCHOLOGY
STATISTICS
STRENGTH OF MATERIALS &
   MECHANICS OF SOLIDS
TECHNICAL DESIGN GRAPHICS
THERMODYNAMICS
TOPOLOGY
TRANSPORT PHENOMENA
VECTOR ANALYSIS

If you would like more information about any of these books,
complete the coupon below and return it to us or visit your local bookstore.

RESEARCH & EDUCATION ASSOCIATION
61 Ethel Road W. • Piscataway, New Jersey 08854
Phone: (732) 819-8880   **website: www.rea.com**

Please send me more information about your Problem Solver books

Name _____

Address _____

City _____ State _____ Zip _____